WHY DOES MY BODY DO THAT?

BLINK

by Rachel Rose

Consultant: Beth Gambro
Reading Specialist, Yorkville, Illinois

Minneapolis, Minnesota

Teaching Tips

Before Reading

- Look at the cover of the book. Discuss the picture and the title.

- Ask readers to brainstorm a list of what they already know about blinking. What can they expect to see in this book?

- Go on a picture walk, looking through the pictures to discuss vocabulary and make predictions about the text.

During Reading

- Read for purpose. Encourage readers to think about blinking as they are reading.

- Ask readers to look for the details of the book. What are they learning about the body and how it blinks?

- If readers encounter an unknown word, ask them to look at the sounds in the word. Then, ask them to look at the rest of the page. Are there any clues to help them understand?

After Reading

- Encourage readers to pick a buddy and reread the book together.

- Ask readers to name two reasons why the body blinks. Find the pages that tell about these things.

- Ask readers to write or draw something they learned about blinks.

Credits: Cover and title page, © kibler/Shutterstock; 3, © Master1305/Shutterstock; 5, © LeManna/iStock and © Suzanne Tucker/Shutterstock; 6–7, © Rawpixel.com/Shutterstock and © Rawpixel.com/Shutterstock; 8, © SciePro/Shutterstock; 9, © alexei_tm/iStock; 11, © Alexander Klunnikov/Shutterstock; 12–13, © kiankhoon/iStock; 14–15, © p_ponomareva/iStock and © KatarzynaBialasiewicz/iStock; 17, © kohei_hara/iStock; 18–19, © SDI Productions/iStock; 20–21, © shapecharge/iStock and © Valeriya/iStock; 22, © Tetiana Lazunova/iStock; 23TL, © libre de droit/iStock; 23TC, © BlackJack3D/iStock; 23TR, © SDI Productions/iStock; 23BL, © fizkes/iStock; 23BC, © Hakase_/iStock; and 23BR, © RichLegg/iStock.

Library of Congress Cataloging-in-Publication Data

Names: Rose, Rachel, 1968- author.
Title: Blink / by Rachel Rose.
Description: Minneapolis, Minnesota : Bearport Publishing Company, [2023] |
  Series: Why does my body do that? | Includes bibliographical references
  and index.
Identifiers: LCCN 2022027908 (print) | LCCN 2022027909 (ebook) | ISBN
  9798885093347 (library binding) | ISBN 9798885094566 (paperback) | ISBN
  9798885095716 (ebook)
Subjects: LCSH: Eyelids--Juvenile literature. |
  Eyelids--Movements--Juvenile literature.
Classification: LCC QP327 .R67 2023 (print) | LCC QP327 (ebook) | DDC
  612.8/47--dc23/eng/20220729
LC record available at https://lccn.loc.gov/2022027908
LC ebook record available at https://lccn.loc.gov/2022027909

Copyright © 2023 Bearport Publishing Company. All rights reserved. No part of this publication may be reproduced in whole or in part, stored in any retrieval system, or transmitted in any form or by any means, electronic, mechanical, photocopying, recording, or otherwise, without written permission from the publisher.

For more information, write to Bearport Publishing, 5357 Penn Avenue South, Minneapolis, MN 55419.

Contents

Staring Game 4

See It Happen 22

Glossary 23

Index 24

Read More 24

Learn More Online 24

About the Author 24

Staring Game

I play a game with my friend.

We **stare** into each other's eyes.

Who will blink first?

I do!

Why does my body do that?

A blink is when your eyes shut and open quickly.

Everybody blinks.

How does it happen?

Your **brain** sends a message to your eyes.

Muscles around the eyes make them close and open.

This quick close and open keeps your eyes safe.

It helps **tears** cover your eyes.

The tears wash away dust and **germs**.

Tears also stop your eyes from getting too dry.

They keep your eyes healthy.

Usually, you blink without thinking about it.

You may not even notice it.

Most people blink about 15 times every minute!

You can also make yourself blink.

Try doing this when your eyes feel tired.

It may make them feel better.

Sometimes, people blink a lot.

You may blink more often when you are surprised.

Being **nervous** can make you blink a lot, too.

People blink all the time.

It is a healthy thing to do.

See if you notice the next time you blink!

See It Happen

The brain sends a message to your eyes.

Muscles make your eyes close.

Then, the muscles make your eyes open again.

Glossary

brain the part of the body that tells the other parts what to do

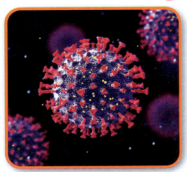

germs tiny living things that can make people sick

muscles parts of the body that help you move

nervous worried or scared

stare to look at something nonstop

tears water in and around your eyes

Index

brain 8, 22
dust 10
germs 10
muscles 8, 22
staring 4
tears 10, 12

Read More

Berne, Emma Carlson. *Let's Explore the Sense of Sight (Discover Your Senses).* Minneapolis: Lerner Publications, 2020.

Hansen, Grace. *Eye Gunk (Beginning Science: Gross Body Functions).* Minneapolis: Abdo Kids, 2021.

Learn More Online

1. Go to **www.factsurfer.com** or scan the QR code below.
2. Enter "**Blink**" into the search box.
3. Click on the cover of this book to see a list of websites.

About the Author

Rachel Rose liked playing staring games when she was a child, but she usually blinked and lost!